KU-676-163

Under the Official Secrets Act 1989, Chapter 6, subsection 1, a person who is or has been:

> (a) a member of the security and intelligence services; or
>
> (b) notified that he is subject to the provisions of this subsection

is guilty of an offence if without lawful authority he discloses any information, document or other article relating to security or intelligence which is or has been in his possession by virtue of his position as a member of any of those services or in the course of his work while the notification is or was in force.

I hereby agree to abide by the provisions of the Act.

Signature_____ Date_____

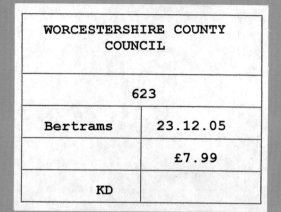

This is a work of fiction. Names, characters, places and incidents are either the product of the author's imagination or, if real, are used fictitiously.

First published 2005 by Walker Books Ltd, 87 Vauxhall Walk, London SE11 5HJ

10 9 8 7 6 5 4 3 2 1

Text © 2005 Anthony Horowitz

Illustrations © 2005 John Lawson

Alex Rider Icon™ © 2005 Walker Books Ltd

The right of Anthony Horowitz and John Lawson to be identified as author and illustrator respectively of this work has been asserted by them in accordance with the Copyright, Designs and Patents Act 1988

All photographs © Science Photo Library and individuals as credited below:
p.8, Volker Steger; p.11, Sheila Terry; p.12 left, Andrew Lambert Photography; p.12 right, Jim Stoots, Lawrence Livermore National Laboratory; p.14, Martyn F. Chillmaid; p.15, Alfred Pasieka; p.16, Sandia National Laboratories; p.17, Sidney Moulds; p.19, Dr Peter Harris; p.20 left, Chris Knapton; p.20 right, Lawrence Lawry; p.22 left, Dr Gary Settles; p.22 right, Charles D. Winters; p.24 left, Alexander Tsiaras; p.24 right, Mehau Kulyk; p.26, Dr Tony Brain; p.27, American Science & Engineering; p.29, Dr Jeremy Burgess; p.30, Geoff Williams; p.31, Philippe Plailly; p.32, Geoff Tompkinson; p.34, Science Photo Library; p.35, Jerry Mason; p.36, Dale Boyer; p.38 left, Charles D. Winters; p.38 right, Tom McHugh; p.41, Gusto; p.42, Victor Habbick Visions.

This book has been typeset in ITC Officina Sans Book

Printed in China

British Library Cataloguing in Publication Data:
a catalogue record for this book is available from the British Library

ISBN 1-84428-116-7

www.alexrider.com
www.walkerbooks.co.uk

ANTHONY HOROWITZ

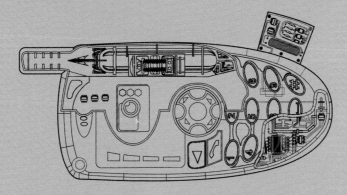

ALEX RIDER
THE GADGETS

TECHNICAL RESEARCHER: Emil Fortune

TECHNICAL ILLUSTRATOR: John Lawson

WALKER BOOKS

AND SUBSIDIARIES

LONDON • BOSTON • SYDNEY • AUCKLAND

Introduction

From: Smithers (Covert Weapons Section)
To: Alan Blunt (CE Special Operations, MI6)
Subject: Dossier

I have received your request for a breakdown of all devices used by Alex Rider on his first five missions.

If I may say so, and with the greatest respect, I am rather baffled. What is it, I wonder, that you wish to do with this dossier? I need hardly remind you of the trouble with dossiers that we at MI6 have had in the past!

I am very concerned that the hard work undertaken by my department may fall into the wrong hands. Organizations such as Scorpia (to name but one) would have a keen interest in knowing what we get up to here. But even our American friends in the CIA have made no secret of their desire to see our blueprints – simply so they can appropriate them.

If you are going to produce a book of some sort, I would suggest we build in a simple device that will cause it to burst into flames when it is opened. I used just such a trick in a get well card which I sent Alex when he was in hospital after his last mission. I'm told he liked it very much, although the nurses and fire brigade were perhaps less amused.

Or might you at least consider publishing the dossier in code? A simple code such as this, for example:

    1L2   XR3   D2R   3S1   S5P   2RB   4P2   R1T   3V2

Anyway, it is now almost a year since you told me that we might have a fourteen-year-old agent joining us. I have to say, I nearly ate my hat – not difficult in fact as it was manufactured to produce emergency rations in the field. As you requested, however, I began to think of covert weapons (we do insist on calling them "gadgets" – although I've always found the word inappropriate, myself) which might be of use.

This provided a very interesting challenge. You will be familiar with some of our recent successes. The exploding briefcase, X-ray video camera, semi-automatic golf clubs and toxic aftershave have all become standard issue. I am particularly proud of the Palm Organizer which we converted to become a miniature flame-thrower. You will recall that we renamed this the Napalm Organizer.

But all of these are only really suitable for adults and you were asking me to equip a fourteen-year-old boy! And so, when I began devising weapons for Alex Rider I had to start with this question. What would a teenager be likely to have in his pockets – apart, that is, from his hands? It is fortunate that I have a nephew of the same age as Alex and was able to take a quick peek in his bedroom – this gave me the inspiration for the devices which you will find described on the pages that follow.

My nephew has at one time or another owned a hand-held games console, a yo-yo, a tube of zit cream, a bicycle, a Harry Potter novel (although I'm afraid he never finished it), a personal CD player, a mobile phone and a packet of bubblegum. I have managed to turn all of these everyday objects into serviceable weapons.

I wonder, by the way, if you might ever consider sending a young female agent into action? I have, for example, developed a very pretty doll that cries, wets itself and then blows up. My department is also working on a bracelet where every item on the chain produces a different toxic gas when dissolved in water. Not so much a charm bracelet as a harm bracelet, we like to think.

One very tricky problem we have had to confront is your insistence that all Alex's weapons should be non-lethal. For example, when we sent Alex to Skeleton Key, he was equipped with a model five mobile phone (the aerial was actually a stun dart which could be fired at a range of up to twenty metres) rather than the far more dangerous model seven, which blows up when you dial unless it is held upside down. This model is known as a "hands free", as many enemy agents who have tried to use it have indeed found themselves free of any hands.

Another example is the keyring that Alex used to escape from General Sarov at Edinburgh Airport. Like the model five phone, this device contained a fairly harmless stun grenade instead of something more dangerous. The enemy was knocked out but recovered all too quickly, and as a result Alex was recaptured.

My Rubik's Cube hand grenade was also rejected by you, you may remember, although I admit that this was not one of my department's greatest successes, as you had to line up all the colours to arm the thing, which could take days.

Nonetheless, I have to say that I am puzzled by your attitude. I hardly need remind you that Alex has confronted some of the most dangerous criminals in the world. Herod Sayle, Dr Grief, General Sarov, Damian Cray – none of them would think twice before killing him. Most of them, in fact, wouldn't think once. But he is only ever allowed to knock them out!

I know Alex is a juvenile. But he has always struck me as being a very level-headed boy ... the sort of boy who would never strike anyone, in fact, except in self-defence. I have spoken to the Armoury Section and they are also keen to equip him. They have suggested a third generation 9mm Smith & Wesson, for example. Something simple to get him started. Can we discuss this at our next inter-departmental meeting?

For your interest, I have included some of the weaponry that was not developed by my department. The Geiger counter games console, for example, was created by the CIA. To my mind, our own Geiger counter (concealed in an electric toothbrush) is more effective. But it's revealing to know what our associates are up to.

For the same reason, I have outlined several of the devices invented by Scorpia. I was particularly struck by the fake pizza which Alex was given. Actually, it's lucky I wasn't struck by it as the thermite charges disguised as olives could have been deadly. They also found an ingenious way to conceal a Kahr P9 double-action semi-automatic in a bottle of soft drink.

There is no doubt that Scorpia scientists – in particular the late Dr Liebermann – came within an inch of killing many thousands of children in London. We need to look more closely at the whole, terrifying world of nanotechnology.

It has been a very rare pleasure and a privilege to prepare Alex Rider for his first five missions and, although I do worry about the boy, you can be assured that I and my department will continue to do everything in our power to keep him safe.

Smithers

Contents

Cutter CD Player

When Alex was sent to infiltrate the mysterious Point Blanc Academy, gadgets were a problem. The only piece of electronic equipment Alex was allowed to take was a personal CD player – as long as all his CDs were classical! So Smithers' CD player works just like the real thing – except for two important secret features...

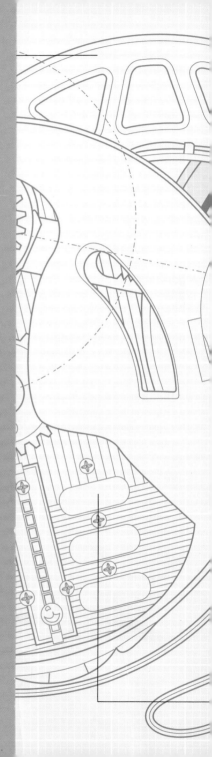

Cutter CD player: This CD player becomes a circular saw when the Beethoven CD is inserted. The saw blade has been manufactured to look and feel as much like a CD as possible. It is a lightweight titanium steel disc with a clear plastic coating on each side and a diamond cutting edge.

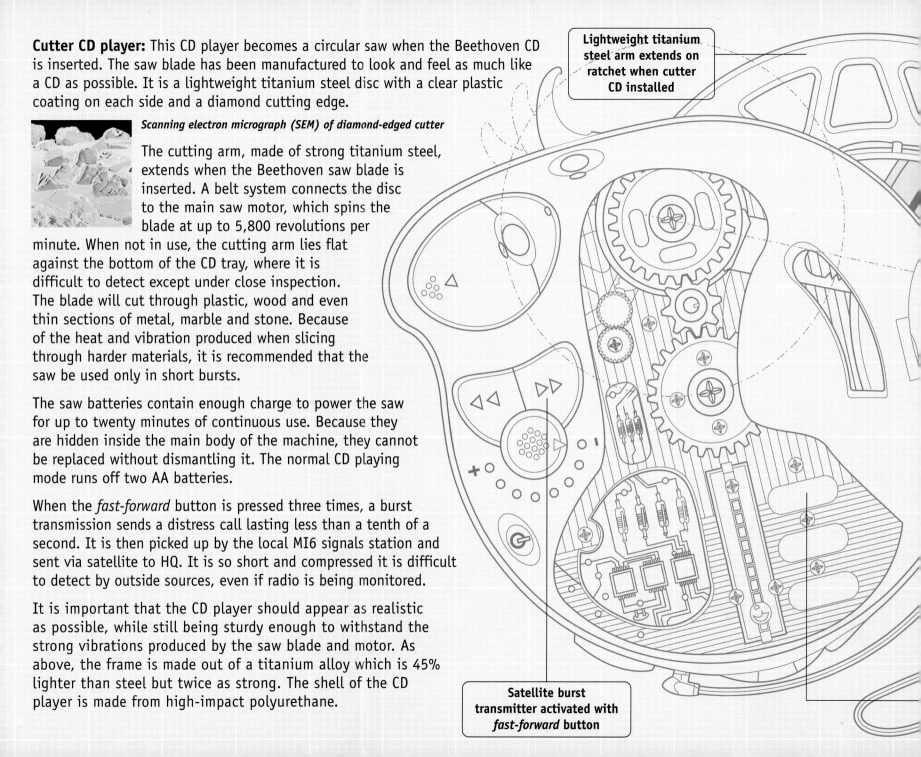

Scanning electron micrograph (SEM) of diamond-edged cutter

The cutting arm, made of strong titanium steel, extends when the Beethoven saw blade is inserted. A belt system connects the disc to the main saw motor, which spins the blade at up to 5,800 revolutions per minute. When not in use, the cutting arm lies flat against the bottom of the CD tray, where it is difficult to detect except under close inspection. The blade will cut through plastic, wood and even thin sections of metal, marble and stone. Because of the heat and vibration produced when slicing through harder materials, it is recommended that the saw be used only in short bursts.

The saw batteries contain enough charge to power the saw for up to twenty minutes of continuous use. Because they are hidden inside the main body of the machine, they cannot be replaced without dismantling it. The normal CD playing mode runs off two AA batteries.

When the *fast-forward* button is pressed three times, a burst transmission sends a distress call lasting less than a tenth of a second. It is then picked up by the local MI6 signals station and sent via satellite to HQ. It is so short and compressed it is difficult to detect by outside sources, even if radio is being monitored.

It is important that the CD player should appear as realistic as possible, while still being sturdy enough to withstand the strong vibrations produced by the saw blade and motor. As above, the frame is made out of a titanium alloy which is 45% lighter than steel but twice as strong. The shell of the CD player is made from high-impact polyurethane.

Lightweight titanium steel arm extends on ratchet when cutter CD installed

Satellite burst transmitter activated with *fast-forward* button

Contents

Cutter CD Player

When Alex was sent to infiltrate the mysterious Point Blanc Academy, gadgets were a problem. The only piece of electronic equipment Alex was allowed to take was a personal CD player – as long as all his CDs were classical! So Smithers' CD player works just like the real thing – except for two important secret features...

Multifunction games console: This hand-held console not only plays games, but also operates as a smoke grenade, surveillance unit, fax/photocopier and bug detector, depending on which cartridge is inserted.

Built into the console body is a microphone, used with the surveillance package to monitor sound. It is sensitive enough to pick up conversations up to one hundred metres away, even behind concrete or metal walls. A set of professional-quality earphones is included with the console, containing miniaturized circuitry to reduce background noise.

Behind the backlit console screen is a single-strip scanning device. This is used to make digital pictures of documents, which are then stored in a 512 MB flash ROM chip. With the correct cartridge installed, the scans can be uploaded and faxed through the telephone port, or printed via a USB printer connection.

All covert functions are accessed by pressing the *start* button three times while the unit is switched on. Otherwise, the console operates as a fully featured 32-bit games machine, with full colour graphics and stereo sound. The life of the built-in rechargeable batteries is up to twenty-five hours when in use, two hundred and fifty in standby mode.

Other cartridges in development for future missions include a version of MI6's latest code-breaking software, designed to crack the block ciphers used in encrypted email; a sophisticated voice-stress analysis package, for use as a lie detector; and an electromagnetic pulse generator, which can be used to destroy all electronic circuitry within a twenty-metre radius.

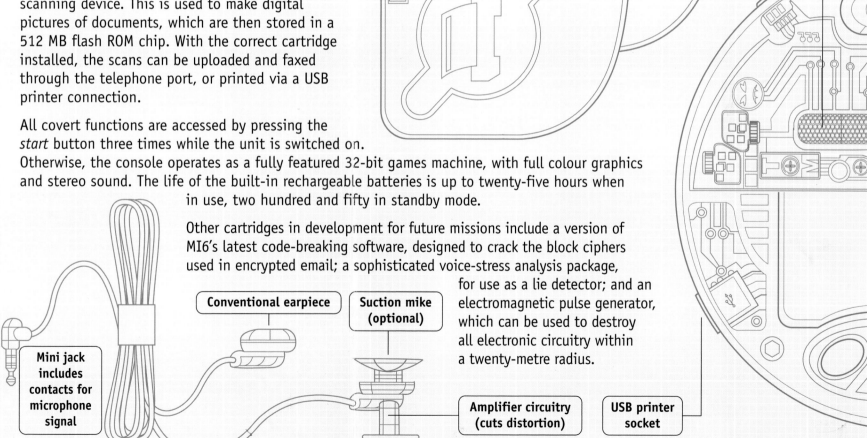

Modem jack

Start button

Microphone

Additional cartridges

Conventional earpiece

Suction mike (optional)

Mini jack includes contacts for microphone signal

Amplifier circuitry (cuts distortion)

USB printer socket

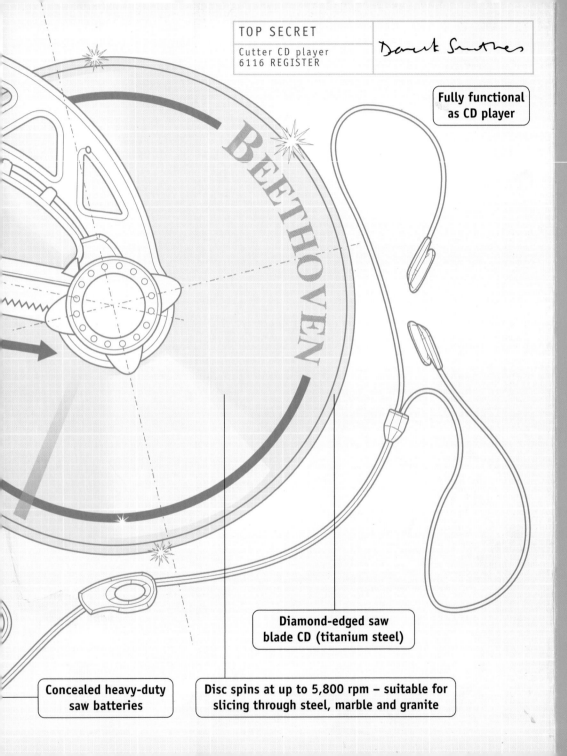

Fully functional
as CD player

BEETHOVEN

Diamond-edged saw
blade CD (titanium steel)

Concealed heavy-duty
saw batteries

Disc spins at up to 5,800 rpm – suitable for
slicing through steel, marble and granite

Multifunction Games Console [1]

The MI6 multifunction games console was developed specially for Alex to take with him to Port Tallon, the home of Herod Sayle's Stormbreaker computer factory. As well as playing games it was designed to copy documents, set off a smoke bomb, detect bugs and see through walls.

Geiger counter games console: Inside this hand-held games console is a Geiger-Müller tube, which detects and measures levels of radioactivity. It is activated by pressing the *play* button three times.

The tube contains a mixture of two gases – neon with a very small amount of halogen – which does not conduct electricity unless it is ionized by a radioactive particle passing through it. When this happens, a current passes between two electrodes inside the tube, and the device turns this into sound. The more radiation that is picked up, the louder and more high-pitched the noise. The screens display the amount of radioactivity detected as green or white flashes.

If the sound produced becomes a constant, high-pitched buzzing, and the screen is entirely white, the user is advised to leave the area immediately, as levels are dangerously high.

CIA | Central Intelligence Agency Blueprint
Authorized:
Dr Keith Messer *Dr Keith Messer*

Geiger-Müller tube

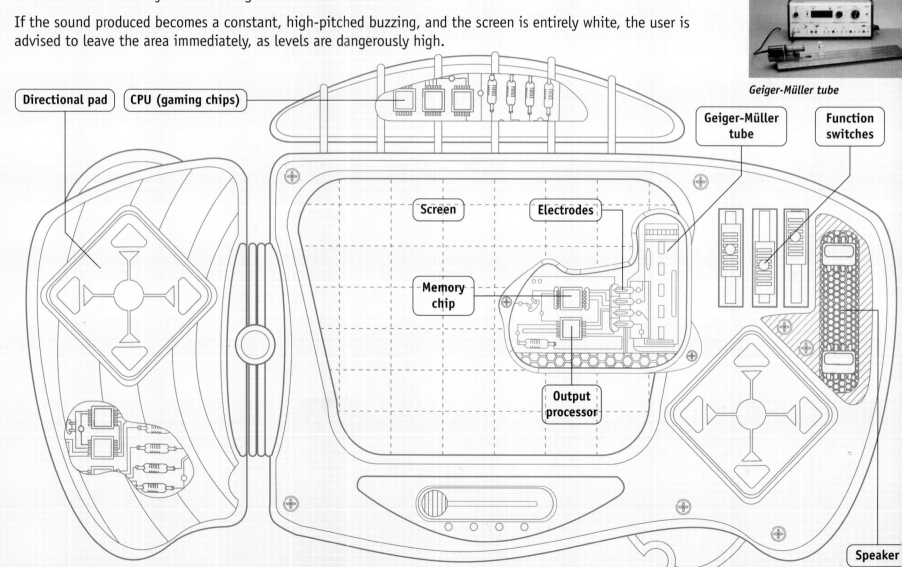

Directional pad

CPU (gaming chips)

Geiger-Müller tube

Function switches

Screen

Electrodes

Memory chip

Output processor

Speaker

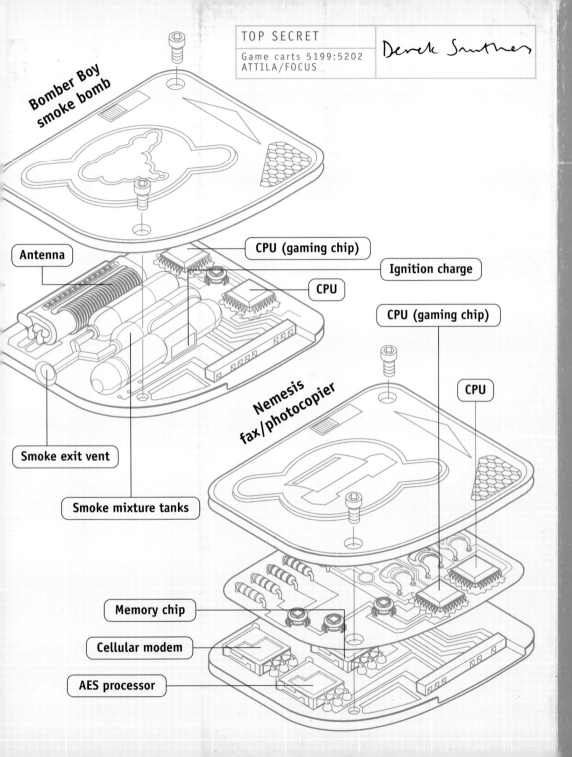

Bomber Boy smoke bomb

Antenna

CPU (gaming chip)

Ignition charge

CPU

CPU (gaming chip)

CPU

Nemesis fax/photocopier

Smoke exit vent

Smoke mixture tanks

Memory chip

Cellular modem

AES processor

Geiger Counter Games Console [CIA Issue]

The CIA gave Alex a games console when he went to work for them in Cuba – but what they didn't tell him was that it contained a Geiger counter to help them find a nuclear bomb. Alex discovered its secret function when it picked up the radiation produced by the luminous face on his hotel alarm clock.

Exocet X-ray and audio amplifier: Known informally at MI6 as "the X-ray cartridge", this is actually a miniaturized ultra wide-band radar device. It has two functions. Firstly, sophisticated signal-processing software allows the console to show clear images of objects on the other side of sheet metal, or the very thickest walls – even those made of steel-reinforced concrete. Secondly, included in the case of the console is a directional microphone, which can pick up conversations up to one thousand metres away. Noise- and volume-filtering software is built in to increase clarity and prevent ear damage.

Speed Wars bug finder: This cartridge is an RF probe which finds the variations in the electromagnetic field caused by antennas and other forms of electronic bugging devices. It is sensitive enough to detect even the lowest powered systems.

Bomber Boy smoke bomb: This cartridge contains a simple 60/40 mixture of potassium nitrate and sugar, melted together. The mixture is ignited electrically when the *start* button is pressed three times, and produces a thick cloud of grey smoke in under two seconds. The smoke is harmless when inhaled.

Potassium nitrate crystals

Nemesis fax/photocopier: When this cartridge is inserted and a document held in front of the screen, the console acts as a digital scanner. A light illuminates the document, and the whole unit is then passed across its surface to produce a photographic-quality colour image which is stored in the internal memory chip. Connecting the console to a printer enables copies to be made of the document; alternatively it can be sent as a fax via any local mobile phone network or landline.

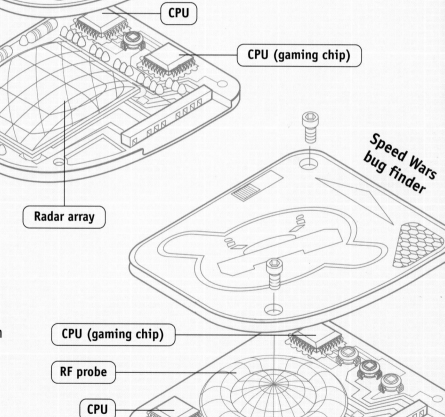

Exocet X-ray and audio amplifier cartridge

Miniature radar chip

CPU

CPU (gaming chip)

Radar array

Speed Wars bug finder

CPU (gaming chip)

RF probe

CPU

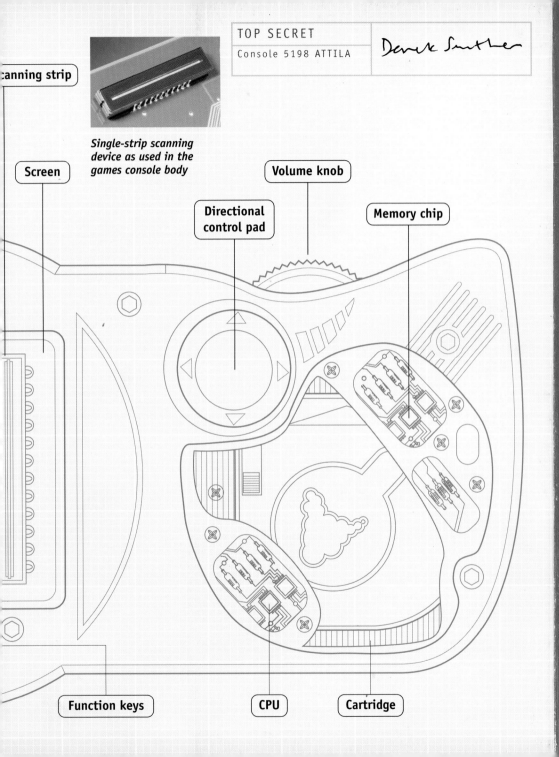

scanning strip

Screen

Single-strip scanning device as used in the games console body

Volume knob

Directional control pad

Memory chip

Function keys

CPU

Cartridge

Multifunction Games Console [2]

Exocet cartridge

Speed Wars cartridge

Bomber Boy cartridge

Nemesis cartridge

High-tensile yo-yo: This black plastic yo-yo, slightly larger than standard, is in fact a miracle of miniaturized engineering. When it is activated using a concealed switch, it acts as a winch, winding the cord back around the axle. It is intended to clip on an agent's belt for use as a climbing aid.

Micromechanical gear arrangement

One half of the yo-yo contains the micromotor array, made from super-tough carbon fibre components bonded together at the molecular level. A complex micromechanical gear system delivers up to 350 watts of power.

The other half houses the highly advanced lanthanum/nickel/tin battery, which supplies as much current as a car battery yet fits into less than a tenth of the space. The battery holds enough charge to let the motor run continuously for one hour. When it is due to be recharged, the agent needs only to use the device as a yo-yo; the spinning motion runs a tiny generator in its core and will charge the unit fully in approximately fifteen minutes.

The shell of the yo-yo, including the belt clip, is made from stress-resistant polycarbonate.

The cord itself is made from an advanced form of nylon that can lift weights of up to one hundred kilograms. Thirty metres of it are wound round the central axle.

Because the yo-yo may have to be used as a toy, either to recharge the battery or to pass inspection, it has been designed to function normally despite the unusually long cord; this has been achieved by using a pair of axles, inner and outer. When the yo-yo is dropped, the cord pays out to a length of one metre before the outer axle locks in place. The two sides can then spin around the inner one. Pulling the cord harder unlocks the outer axle and allows the entire thirty metres to unwind.

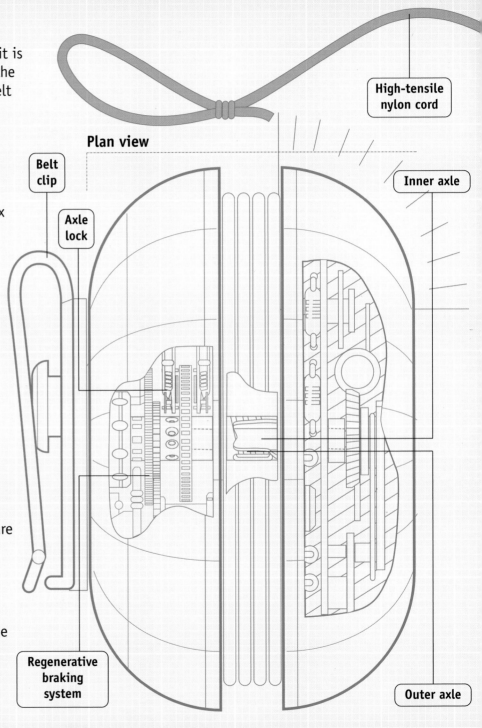

Plan view

High-tensile nylon cord

Belt clip

Axle lock

Inner axle

Regenerative braking system

Outer axle

MI6 Lab Report [1]

From: Smithers (Covert Weapons Section)
To: C Section; Covert Operations; Archives
Subject: Microcapsules

A recent major breakthrough in MI6's Research and Development section has allowed us to produce some exotic and highly useful new equipment.

We have discovered how to conceal a dangerous substance, such as an acid, poison or explosive, inside an entirely innocent one. It will pass any sort of inspection short of detailed chemical analysis, and has a better chance of staying in an agent's possession should he or she be captured or searched. Droplets of the substance are sealed inside microscopic capsules, designed to break open only when they come into contact with specific materials; at all other times they are completely harmless.

For example, we took a commonly available ointment used to prevent spots and added microcapsules of a super-acid: an 80% solution of antimony pentafluoride in hydrofluoric acid. On contact with metal, the acid is released by the action of enzymes, and will rapidly eat through most materials. The ointment is perfectly safe for use on the skin, although we recommend that it should not be swallowed, or applied around metal facial piercings.

We are particularly happy with the bubblegum designed for the agent in the Skeleton Key mission. Concealed in the gum are many microcapsules made of starch which contain a particularly exciting new material: a fullerene foam. When the gum is chewed, the enzyme amylase in saliva breaks down the starch capsules. Fullerene foam is a very strong crystalline lattice of carbon atoms which expands dramatically on contact with air; placed inside a lock or gun barrel it will shatter the metal with ease. (Several batches of the gum were produced and tested. We feel the success of the final product justifies the dental bills.)

Other recent uses of this technology include the high explosive contained in a medicated shampoo. Agents should please stop calling it "Head off Shoulders".

Smithers

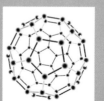

Buckminsterfullerene molecule(C60), a constituent of fullerene foam

High-Tensile Yo-Yo

This hi-tech yo-yo was designed to aid climbing – its powerful winch action and strong cord could lift Alex's weight easily. However, not even Smithers could have foreseen how Alex would use it.

Infrared goggles: The frame of these enhanced goggles is made from extremely tough, durable polyurethane. It is highly resistant to shock, low temperatures and scratching, and so offers ample protection for the delicate electronics contained within. These include the infrared light emitter and head-up display, which combine to give the goggles night-vision capability of up to twenty metres, even on a moonless night.

The light-emitting diode concealed in the frame puts out an impressive 150 milliwatts of infrared light, which is comparable to military-issue infrared torches. It is useful for enhancing infrared vision in low temperature conditions. In order to avoid giving away the night-vision capability, this does not work in the same way as commonly available infrared goggles, in which the wearer looks through two eyepieces at miniature video screens. Here, a pair of concealed low-power lasers on the inside of the frame is used to project the infrared image data directly onto the lenses.

The lenses themselves are a many-layered "sandwich" of different materials. The protective coatings on the outer layer prevent scratching, fogging and icing, and cut down on glare and UV rays for improved visibility and safety in almost all light conditions. The inner layer is coated with a material that glows in laser light, to facilitate the head-up display. Layers of polycarbonate laminate in between give a good deal of resistance to bullets, although this should only be relied upon as a last resort.

The built-in rechargeable battery made of lanthanum, nickel and tin is a great improvement on previous designs, including those commonly used in mobile phones and laptop computers. It holds a charge for much longer, and battery life does not decrease as much with each recharge. Solar panels built into the frame continually trickle-charge the battery when the goggles are exposed to light.

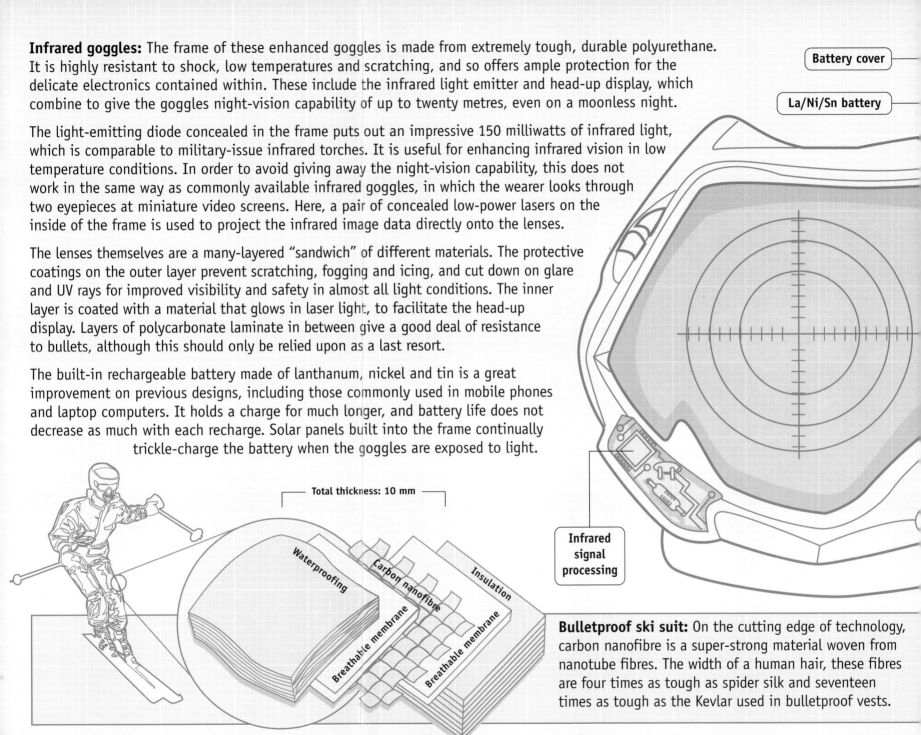

Battery cover

La/Ni/Sn battery

Infrared signal processing

Total thickness: 10 mm

Waterproofing

Carbon nanofibre

Insulation

Breathable membrane

Breathable membrane

Bulletproof ski suit: On the cutting edge of technology, carbon nanofibre is a super-strong material woven from nanotube fibres. The width of a human hair, these fibres are four times as tough as spider silk and seventeen times as tough as the Kevlar used in bulletproof vests.

Polarized light micrograph of nylon fibres

TOP SECRET
Yo-yo 5272 PROOF

Derek Smithers

Side elevation

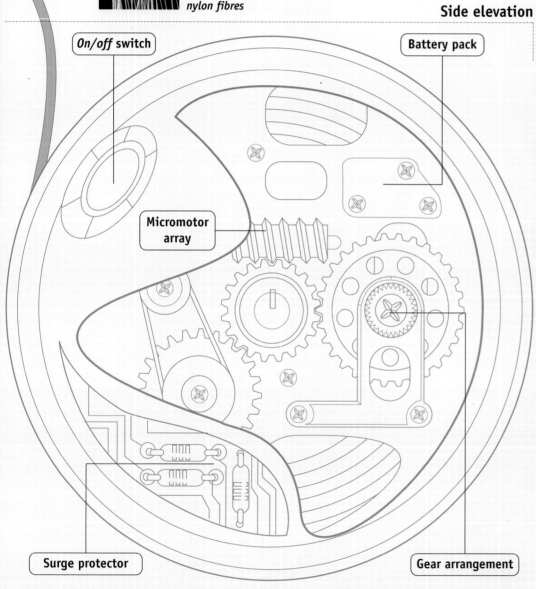

- **On/off switch**
- **Battery pack**
- **Micromotor array**
- **Surge protector**
- **Gear arrangement**

Infrared Goggles and Bulletproof Ski Suit

Point Blanc Academy was perched on the side of a mountain in the French Alps, so it was only natural that Alex would take a ski suit and a pair of goggles with him. As ever, Smithers had made sure that there was more to them than met the eye.

[18]

Exploding ear stud: Outwardly, this appears to be a normal ear stud, with a somewhat large and flashy stone inset. However, it contains a small but powerful explosive charge which can blow a fist-sized hole in virtually any material. Although designed to destroy locks or sabotage machinery, it could serve in an emergency as an anti-personnel device.

The stone consists of a thin crystal shell containing two tiny fluid reservoirs. When separate, the liquids contained in each are completely harmless; when the bomb is armed and they are mixed together, they react with each other to form a binary explosive.

To arm the bomb, the stud is pressed firmly into the butterfly to complete the primary arming circuit. When the two parts are separated again, the secondary arming circuit is completed. The liquids are mixed and a timer counts down from ten seconds, until the trigger circuit detonates the explosive.

The stone is made from diamond-like cubic zirconium crystal, which will shatter on detonation, increasing the device's effectiveness.

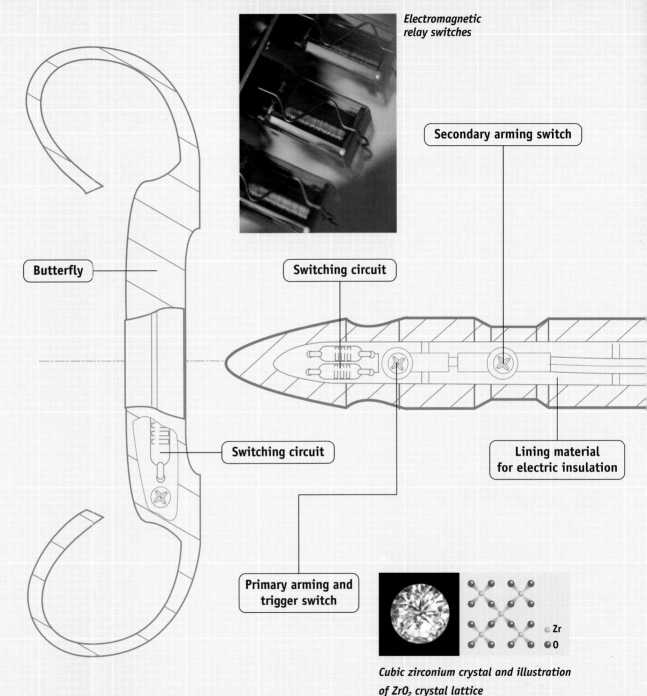

Electromagnetic relay switches

Secondary arming switch

Butterfly

Switching circuit

Switching circuit

Lining material for electric insulation

Primary arming and trigger switch

Zr

O

Cubic zirconium crystal and illustration of ZrO_2 crystal lattice

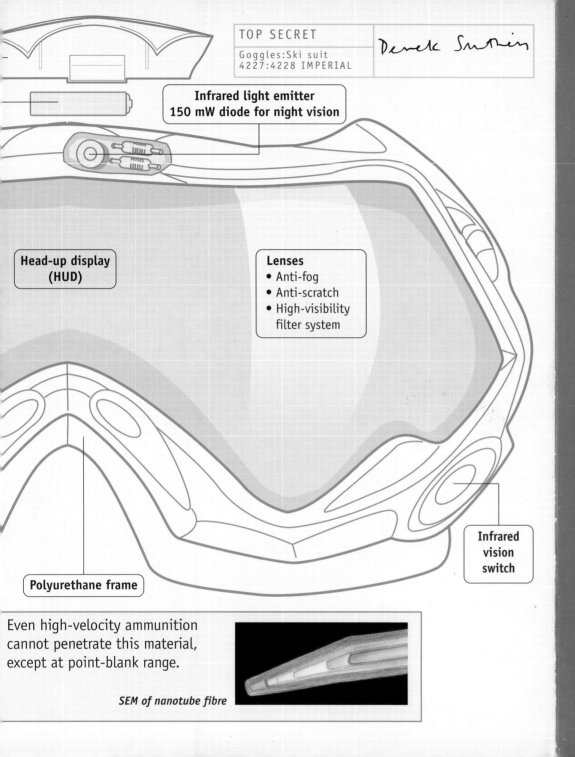

Goggles:Ski suit
4227:4228 IMPERIAL

Derek Smith

Infrared light emitter
150 mW diode for night vision

Head-up display
(HUD)

Lenses
- Anti-fog
- Anti-scratch
- High-visibility
  filter system

Infrared
vision
switch

Polyurethane frame

Even high-velocity ammunition
cannot penetrate this material,
except at point-blank range.

SEM of nanotube fibre

Exploding
Ear Stud

Alex went to Point Blanc Academy
pretending to be spoilt rich kid
Alex Friend, complete with a
pierced ear, a bad reputation and
plenty of attitude. His ear stud,
with its hidden charge of
explosive, helped him avoid
a gruesome fate.

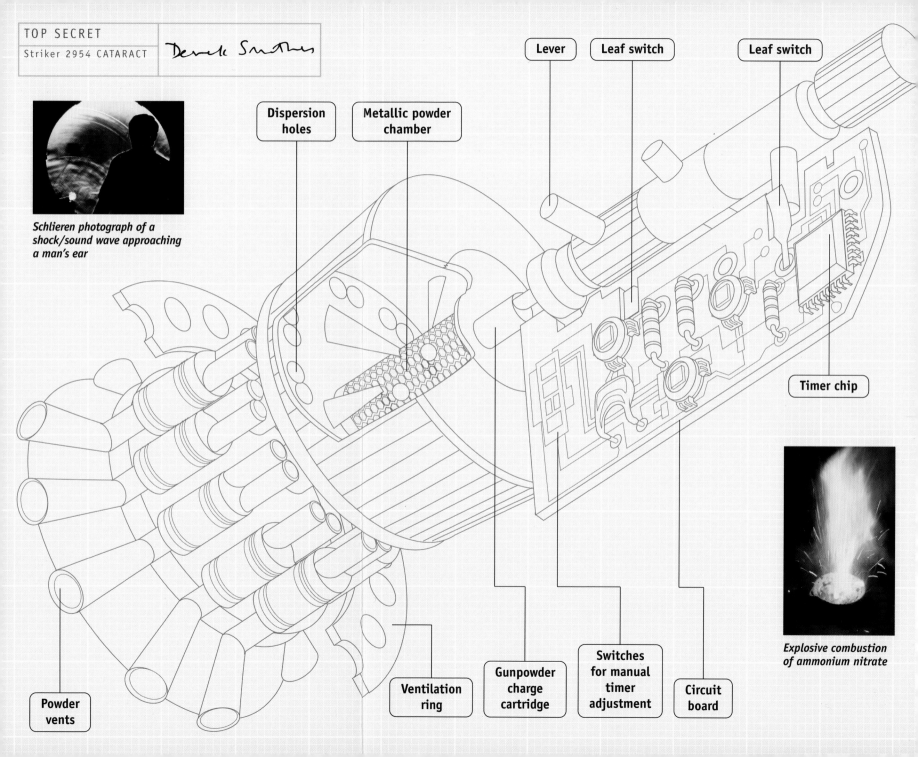

Schlieren photograph of a shock/sound wave approaching a man's ear

Dispersion holes

Metallic powder chamber

Lever

Leaf switch

Leaf switch

Timer chip

Explosive combustion of ammonium nitrate

Powder vents

Ventilation ring

Gunpowder charge cartridge

Switches for manual timer adjustment

Circuit board

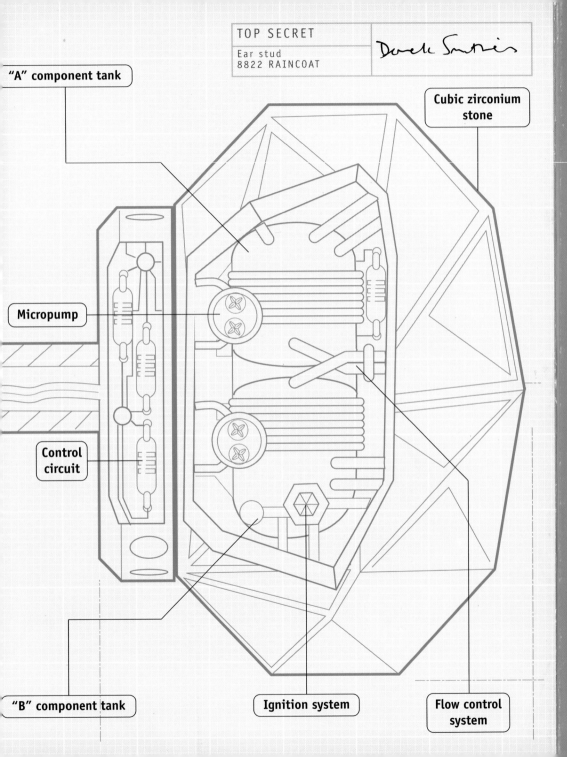

"A" component tank

Micropump

Control circuit

"B" component tank

Cubic zirconium stone

Ignition system

Flow control system

Stun Grenade Keyring

Stun grenades are used by military and law enforcement units all over the world; they explode in a burst of intense light and noise that incapacitates but does not do any lasting damage. Smithers built one into a novelty keyring shaped like a famous footballer; it came in very handy for Alex when the clock was ticking in injury time.

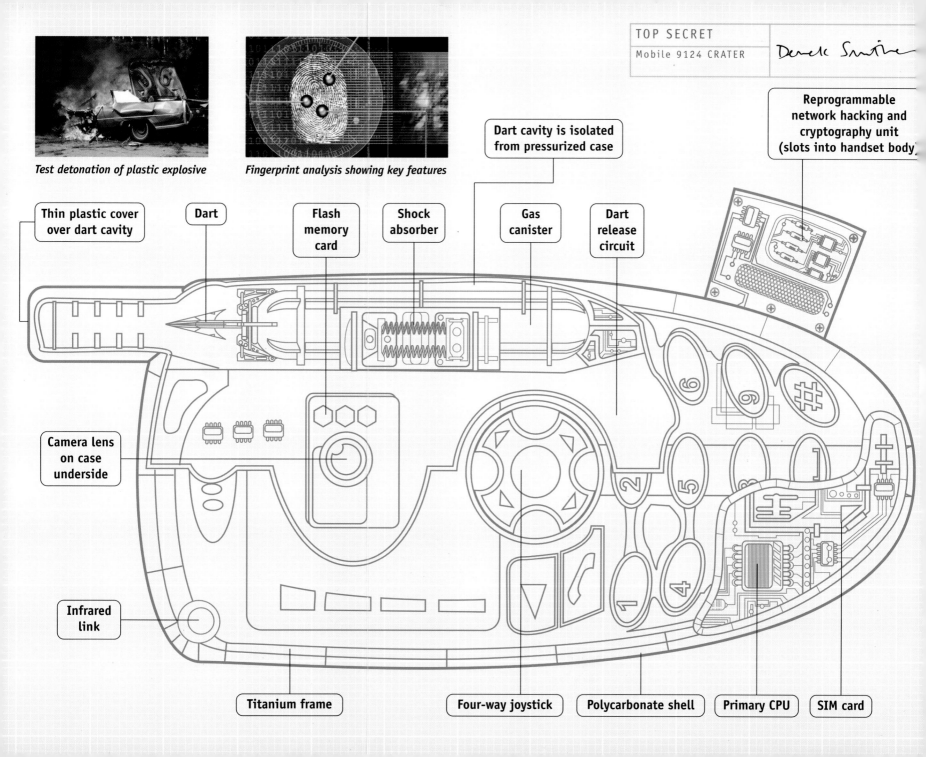

Test detonation of plastic explosive

Fingerprint analysis showing key features

Dart cavity is isolated from pressurized case

Reprogrammable network hacking and cryptography unit (slots into handset body)

Thin plastic cover over dart cavity

Dart

Flash memory card

Shock absorber

Gas canister

Dart release circuit

Camera lens on case underside

Infrared link

Titanium frame

Four-way joystick

Polycarbonate shell

Primary CPU

SIM card

Stun grenade keyring: Known informally as the Striker, this keyring in the shape of a famous footballer is in fact a stun grenade. When the head of the footballer is twisted twice clockwise and once anticlockwise, a ten-second fuse is activated. Then a small charge of gunpowder (2.5 grams) detonates, forcing a burst of metallic particles out of concealed holes in the base of the device. The resulting sheet of dust hangs in the air briefly before combining with oxygen and igniting, creating an explosion. This is non-lethal but will effectively stun anybody in a confined space for several minutes.

The metallic dust is made up of 4.5 grams of a pyrotechnic metal-oxidant mix of magnesium and ammonium powder. The particles burn for less than five hundredths of a second, producing a flash of around 2 million candelas and a bang of around 170 decibels. These levels are low enough not to cause blindness or ruptured eardrums.

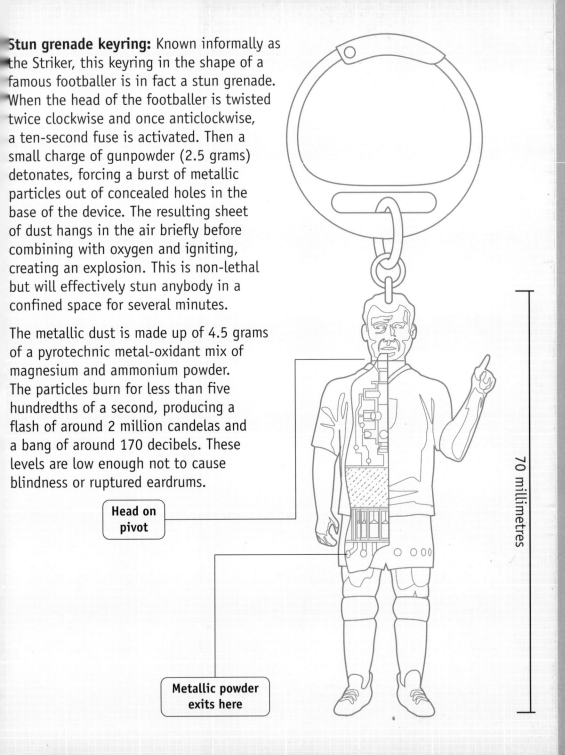

Head on pivot

Metallic powder exits here

70 millimetres

Multifunction Mobile Phone

Alex was sent to work for the CIA – a mission that would take him to Florida, Cuba and even Russia. Wherever he found himself, he could always contact MI6 using this adapted mobile phone, which works all over the world. The phone is impossible to use unless the agent's fingerprint is detected by the keypad, and Alex's model even contained a hidden tranquillizer dart which could be fired out of the aerial – and which Alex used to stunning effect.

Stun-dart book: A flat canister of compressed carbon dioxide gas concealed in the book's spine propels a stun dart when the trigger (the author's name) is pressed hard. The formula of MI6's current rapid-action knockout chemical, RAKO-88, is a closely guarded secret. It causes unconsciousness in a matter of seconds; this lasts up to one hour and has no serious side effects, although headaches and temporary nausea have been reported. An early knockout book design simply reads out extracts from GCSE set texts. This has been banned under the Geneva Convention.

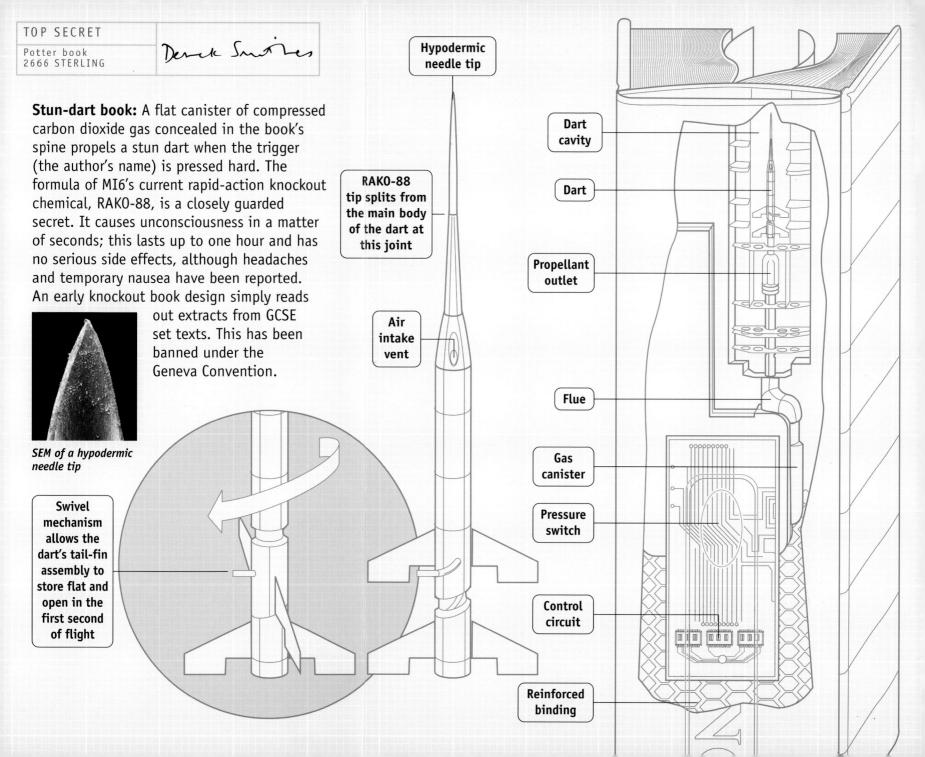

SEM of a hypodermic needle tip

Hypodermic needle tip

RAKO-88 tip splits from the main body of the dart at this joint

Air intake vent

Swivel mechanism allows the dart's tail-fin assembly to store flat and open in the first second of flight

Dart cavity

Dart

Propellant outlet

Flue

Gas canister

Pressure switch

Control circuit

Reinforced binding

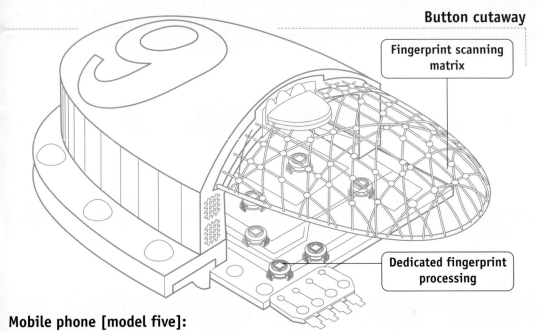

Fingerprint scanning matrix

Dedicated fingerprint processing

Stun-Dart Book

Alex is never issued with lethal weapons on his missions, but on occasion he needs to be able to knock an enemy out from a distance. Smithers designed this stun-dart book to help him do this quickly and quietly.

It was a surprise to everyone when Alex was forced to use it not on a guard or an assassin, but on a fifteen-year-old girl.

Mobile phone [model five]:
This modified mobile phone provides a direct link to MI6 headquarters from any location in the world with network service. Sophisticated telephone network hacking routines mean that the calls are untraceable and encrypted to prevent eavesdropping; tracking the phone location is only possible if the correct security codes are known. The entire case, which is made of lightweight, high-impact substances such as titanium steel, ABS resin and polycarbonate, is sealed and pressurized. It will therefore work underwater to depths of eighty metres and even in the vacuum of space (although the user may have difficulty getting a signal). The phone keypad is fingerprint-sensitive and restricted to the designated user. Unauthorized use is impossible. In the latest versions of the model five, the core of the aerial is in fact a stun dart tipped with RAKO-88, which is shot out by a compressed gas cylinder on dialling 999. The effective range is twenty metres. RAKO-88 causes unconsciousness in a matter of seconds; this lasts up to one hour and has no serious side effects, although headaches and temporary nausea have been reported.

Mobile phone [model seven]: This model has the added features of a mercury switch and a small charge of plastic explosive; unless the phone is held upside down when dialling, it will explode as soon as the call connects.

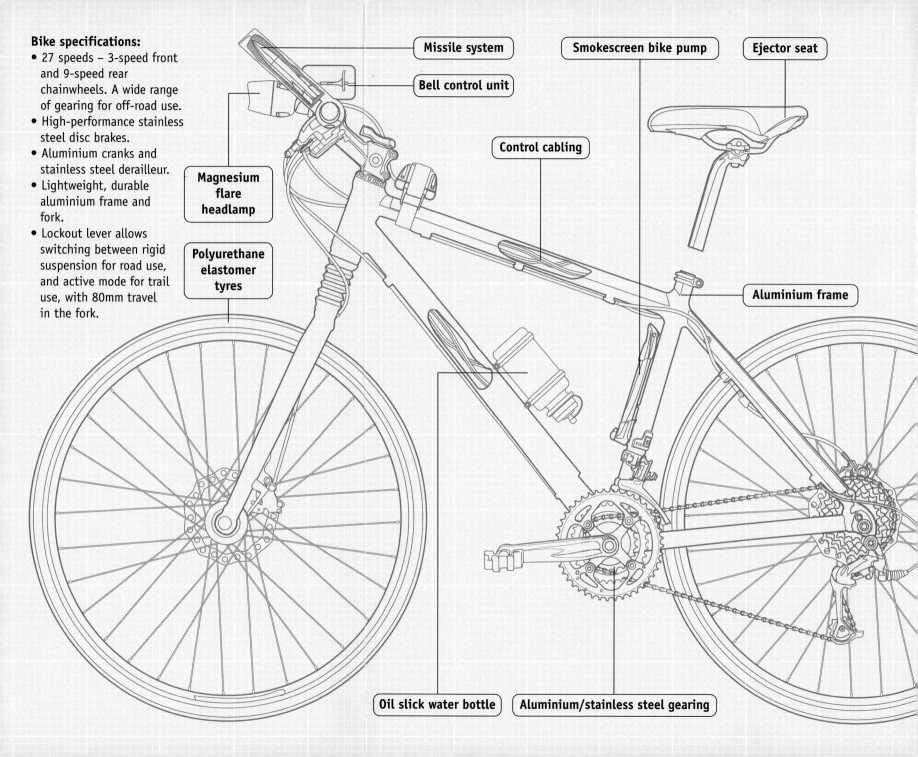

Bike specifications:

- 27 speeds – 3-speed front and 9-speed rear chainwheels. A wide range of gearing for off-road use.
- High-performance stainless steel disc brakes.
- Aluminium cranks and stainless steel derailleur.
- Lightweight, durable aluminium frame and fork.
- Lockout lever allows switching between rigid suspension for road use, and active mode for trail use, with 80mm travel in the fork.

Missile system

Bell control unit

Smokescreen bike pump

Ejector seat

Magnesium flare headlamp

Control cabling

Polyurethane elastomer tyres

Aluminium frame

Oil slick water bottle

Aluminium/stainless steel gearing

MI6 Lab Report [2]

From: Smithers (Covert Weapons Section)
To: C Section; Covert Operations; Archives
Subject: Project Aegis

Project Aegis was created to research new methods of protecting and assisting staff in embassies and MI6 offices worldwide. The first test systems have been installed in my offices at Liverpool Street and are performing extremely well.

It is vital to be able to check people visiting these offices for weapons and other smuggled material. You may be aware that there is specialized machinery built into the lifts for just that reason. However, we have recently been looking into ultra wide-band radar devices that will fit on a desk. The final version, which is disguised as an anglepoise lamp, has been shown to be highly effective. It tracks human beings by body heat, using its millimetre-wavelength radar antenna to detect objects through clothing. The scanner can see all the way through to the human skeleton, and has resolution fine enough to read the text on coins and credit cards. The output can be connected to a PC so that the user can search a guest thoroughly without his or her knowledge.

Document security is always a concern. Shredders are bulky and not entirely efficient, so we have researched new methods of destroying papers. The out-tray on my desk contains powerful electric terminals which can disintegrate a document thoroughly in a matter of seconds, with no flame and very little smoke.

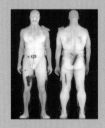

Weapons detection scan

Two concealed lifts have been built into my office. One is connected to the Research and Development labs, and the other goes to street level (it comes out in the back room of the Prince of Wales pub, which is handy). The first lift is built into the large sofa – the middle seat drops into the floor, and the gap is closed by the seats on either side. The second lift is inside the wall behind the filing cabinet, which splits open to reveal the entrance. We feel this system is ideal for keeping the secure areas of the building secret as well as safe.

Smithers

Cannondale Bad Boy Bike [1]

A bombing in France set Alex on the trail of multimillionaire pop star Damian Cray, but nobody at MI6 would believe him. Nobody, that is, except for Smithers, who sent Alex this modified bicycle – perfect for a chase through the narrow streets of Amsterdam.

Bell control unit: The large old-fashioned bell may appear slightly out of place next to the bicycle's cutting-edge design, but in fact it acts as the control centre for all of its special features. Pressing the lever on the side causes the bell to ring; pulling it makes the top flip up to reveal a set of colour-coded buttons, each of which activates a different device:

orange: missile system *blue:* smokescreen *red:* ejector seat
yellow: magnesium flare *green:* oil slick

Control cables are built into the bicycle frame, linking the devices together.

Handlebar missile system: This is activated by pressing the orange button. The handlebars of the modified Bad Boy contain two heat-seeking missiles, which are designed to disable vehicles. The rear section of each missile contains solid rocket fuel, which is ignited when the control button is pressed. A covering flap at the front of the handlebar springs open, allowing the missile to shoot out at tremendous speed.

During the rocket thrust, a tiny infrared camera in the nose cone senses the hottest thing in the area, and the missile locks on to its target. The camera is tuned to ignore humans in favour of hotter targets, such as vehicle engines and exhaust gases. Once the rocket section has burnt out, the middle section acts as a ramjet: a miniature jet engine through which air is rammed due to its high speed. Because of the limited amount of fuel the missiles carry, ramjet flight time is under ten seconds.

As soon as the ramjet kicks in, the guidance circuitry begins to control the attitude fins at the rear. These fins change the direction of flight and are capable of moving the missile through wide turns in the air.

The nose cone of the missile contains a vent, an impact trigger and thirty grams of powerful plastic explosive which is set off on impact with the target. The trigger is armed by high-speed airflow through the vent so that the explosive cannot be detonated accidentally when the missile is in the firing chamber.

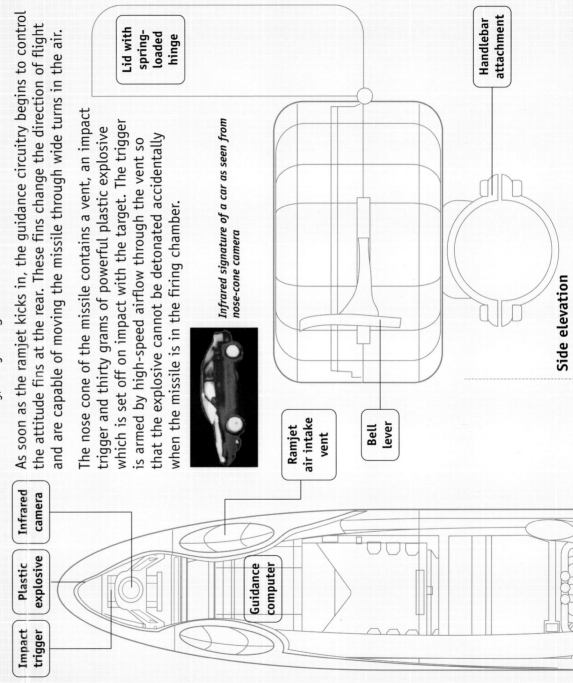

Infrared signature of a car as seen from nose-cone camera

Lid with spring-loaded hinge

Handlebar attachment

Side elevation

Bell lever

Ramjet air intake vent

Impact trigger

Plastic explosive

Infrared camera

Guidance computer

Bike overview: This customized bicycle is designed to provide a fast, safe and reliable means of transport for agents in urban areas.

The aluminium frame has been engineered to be light, strong and shock-absorbent; it will stand up to an impressive amount of punishment and is rigid enough to prevent much energy from being wasted through side-to-side movement. State-of-the-art suspension and gearing make for great comfort, speed and versatility.

The tyres, manufactured using a new polyurethane elastomer technology, cannot be punctured or lose pressure. The insides contain a honeycomb of pressurized cells which are so small that if one or more deflate it makes little difference to the performance of the bicycle. They absorb shock and resist weathering more effectively than standard rubber tyres.

False colour SEM of multicelled polyurethane elastomer

A variety of devices has been built into the bicycle to deter pursuit – a smokescreen, oil dispenser and two heat-seeking missiles – and the seat post acts as an emergency ejection system. There are also accessories for the rider, such as a bulletproof cycle jersey and magnetic bike clips, and an intensely bright magnesium headlamp.

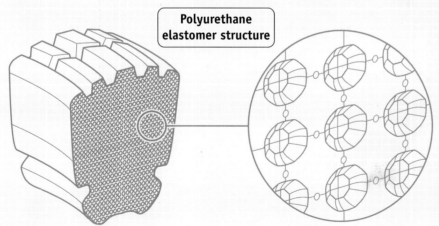

Polyurethane elastomer structure

Cannondale Bad Boy Bike [2]

Bell Control Unit

Handlebar

Missile System

Smokescreen bike pump: This is activated by the blue button. The pump included with the modified Bad Boy does not, in fact, work as a pump; the flat-free tyres should mean that punctures and deflation are never a problem. Instead it contains a miniature smoke machine designed to facilitate evasion of pursuers.

The smoke machine heats a mixture of distilled water and propylene glycol and forces it into the air under pressure. The smoke is dense and non-toxic. Because it is heated it tends to rise slowly; this means that the screen should work to mask the bike rider for thirty seconds before the fluid reservoir runs out, and for a further ten seconds until it disperses. Times may differ in windy conditions.

The heating coil wrapped around the fluid tank will heat the contents to the correct temperature in under one second. The batteries powering it contain enough charge for one use and, like the fluid, must be replaced afterwards.

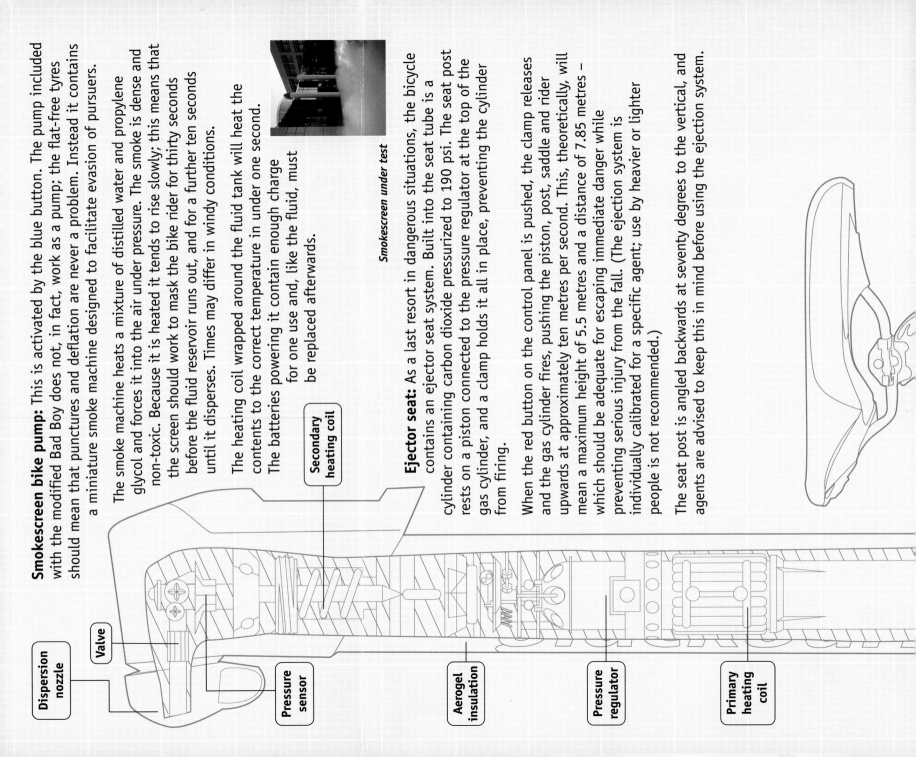

Smokescreen under test

Ejector seat: As a last resort in dangerous situations, the bicycle contains an ejector seat system. Built into the seat tube is a cylinder containing carbon dioxide pressurized to 190 psi. The seat post rests on a piston connected to the pressure regulator at the top of the gas cylinder, and a clamp holds it all in place, preventing the cylinder from firing.

When the red button on the control panel is pushed, the clamp releases and the gas cylinder fires, pushing the piston, post, saddle and rider upwards at approximately ten metres per second. This, theoretically, will mean a maximum height of 5.5 metres and a distance of 7.85 metres – which should be adequate for escaping immediate danger while preventing serious injury from the fall. (The ejection system is individually calibrated for a specific agent; use by heavier or lighter people is not recommended.)

The seat post is angled backwards at seventy degrees to the vertical, and agents are advised to keep this in mind before using the ejection system.

Dispersion nozzle

Valve

Pressure sensor

Secondary heating coil

Aerogel insulation

Pressure regulator

Primary heating coil

Cannondale Bad Boy Bike [3]

Smokescreen

Bike Pump

Ejector Seat

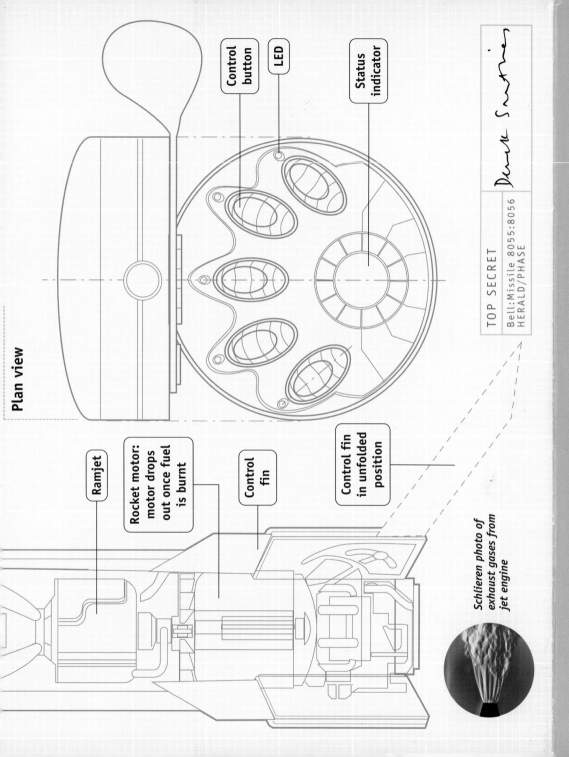

Plan view

Control button

LED

Status indicator

Ramjet

Rocket motor: motor drops out once fuel is burnt

Control fin

Control fin in unfolded position

Schlieren photo of exhaust gases from jet engine

[32]

Magnesium flare headlamp: When the yellow button is pressed, the magnesium flare hidden behind the bulb of the headlamp ignites. In less than one second, it reaches 4,000 degrees Fahrenheit, creating a light of blinding intensity. The inside of the headlamp is sealed and mirrored to prevent dazzling the rider and to direct the beam forward.

Oil slick water bottle: The oil-releasing water bottle is used to prevent pursuit of the agent. It is activated by pressing the green button and is effective against all types of land vehicles and pedestrians.

The oil contained in the bottle is in fact a liquid containing particles of polytetrafluoroethylene (PTFE) – one of the most slippery substances known to man, and often used to coat non-stick saucepans. It is pressurized so that when the control switch is pressed the oil will spray out of the nozzle. The nozzle itself is angled slightly behind and to the side to prevent the oil from affecting the back wheel of the bicycle.

Magnetic bike clips: The four bicycle clips supplied with the modified Bad Boy contain powerful electromagnets. When they are switched on, they each produce a magnetic field strong enough to hold weights of up to one hundred kilograms. The battery life is up to one hour of continuous use.

Bulletproof cycle jersey: The cycle jersey is made from MI6's newest bulletproof nanofibre, and will prevent serious injury from bullets and knives. It should not be relied upon at point-blank range.

Battery pack

Control cable port

Pressure regulator valve

Nozzle

Micropump

Filter system

PTFE liquid chamber

SEM of PTFE tape

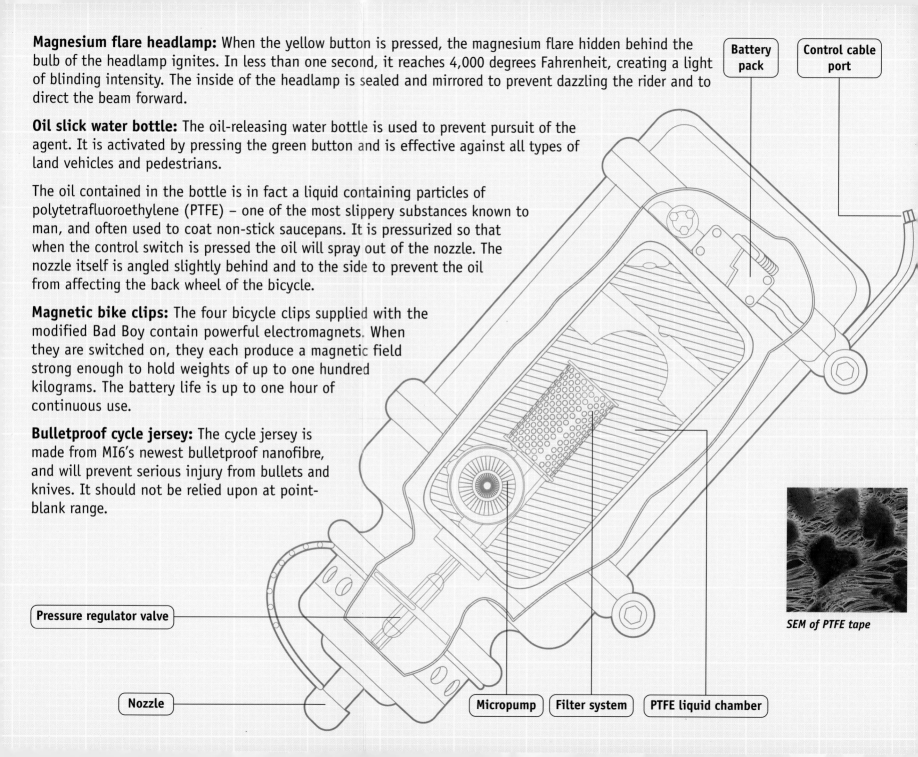

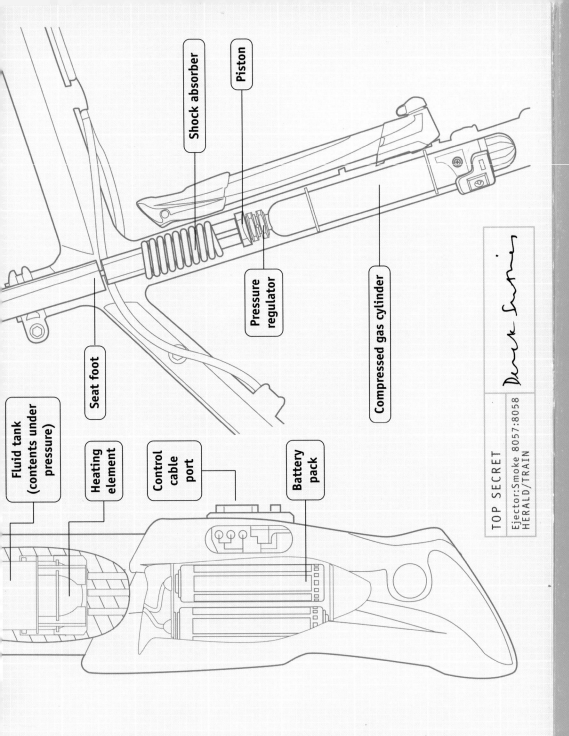

Shock absorber

Piston

Pressure regulator

Compressed gas cylinder

Seat foot

Fluid tank (contents under pressure)

Heating element

Control cable port

Battery pack

TOP SECRET
Ejector:Smoke 8057:8058
HERALD/TRAIN

Cannondale Bad Boy Bike [4]

Magnesium Flare Headlamp

Oil Slick Water Bottle

Magnetic Bike Clips

Bulletproof Cycle Jersey

Radio mouth brace: This brace is a simple and easy-to-use tracking device. The radio transmitter is held on a circuit board printed over the top of the brace, so that it lies against the roof of the mouth. The metal loops which hold it in place act as an aerial.

When it is worn, the brace transmits a steady and powerful signal which is constantly monitored by MI6's network of radio towers. Each tower analyses the direction and strength of the signal, and by putting this information together the location of the wearer can be pinpointed. The accuracy of the system depends on the amount of information available, but it is usually as close as thirty metres.

A tiny switch built into the underside of the brace changes the frequency of the radio signal being produced. This is often used as a distress call.

The brace operates on kinetic power, in the same way as some modern watches. At the back of the device, in a hollow moulded to the roof of the wearer's mouth, is a small, flat box containing a capacitor, a small weight and a microgenerator. As the wearer's head moves, the weight moves back and forth, causing the generator to spin. This produces enough current to keep the capacitor charged and the radio signal transmitting.

Signal tracking dish

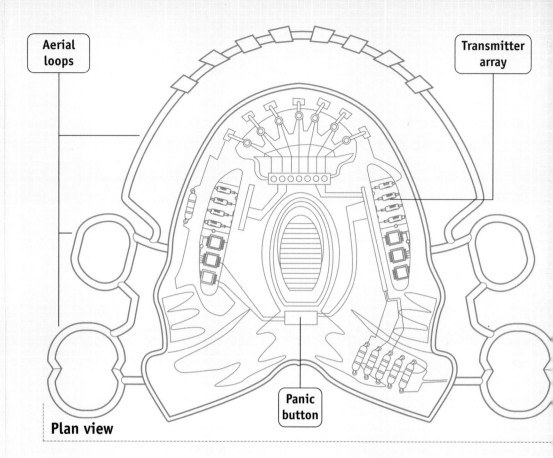

Aerial loops

Transmitter array

Panic button

Plan view

Perspective view

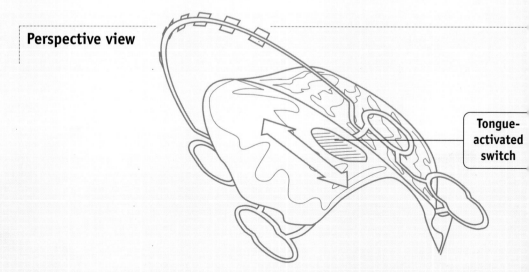

Tongue-activated switch

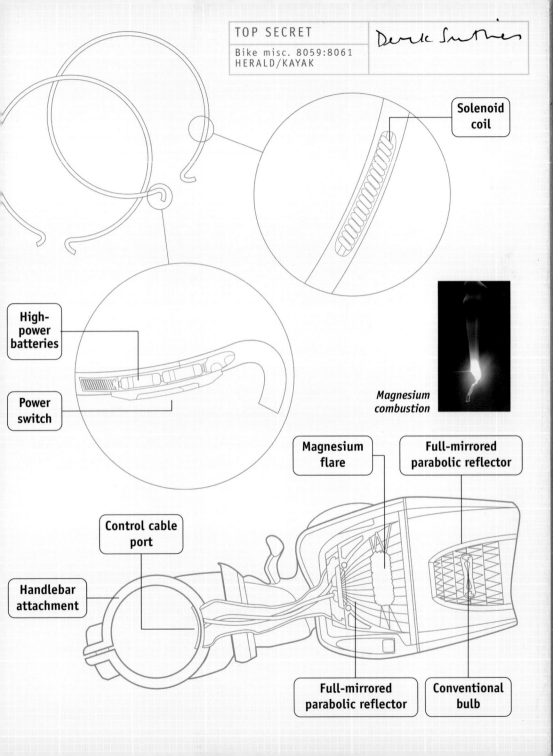

Solenoid
coil

High-
power
batteries

Power
switch

*Magnesium
combustion*

Magnesium
flare

Full-mirrored
parabolic reflector

Control cable
port

Handlebar
attachment

Full-mirrored
parabolic reflector

Conventional
bulb

Radio Mouth Brace

Alex was sent as a double agent to infiltrate the ruthless criminal organization Scorpia. This modified mouth brace, complete with radio transmitter, was designed to allow MI6's strike teams to find him – if he could stay alive long enough.

Blowgun: Scorpia training has often involved the skills of the ninja – the feared spies and assassins of feudal Japan. This blowgun is inspired by the ninja weapon the *fukidake*.

The blowgun is disguised as a drinking straw, and although it is made of slightly more rigid plastic it looks and feels very realistic. The inside of the straw has a low-friction coating to increase range – in the hands of a skilled user, a dart will travel as far as twenty metres. At one end, a special mouthpiece has been inserted to increase the air pressure and prevent the user from accidentally inhaling the dart. Very thin, light darts are supplied with each blowgun. They are made of sharpened wire; if fired into an artery they can be lethal. Some darts are hollow, like hypodermic syringes, and contain drugs or poisons.

The standard-issue Scorpia blowgun is supplied with six darts, colour-coded according to function. Two are standard needle-tipped darts; two contain a fast-acting knockout chemical; and two contain batrachotoxin, a classic blowgun poison of the Colombian rainforest.

Batrachotoxin causes instant paralysis, swiftly followed by death. There is no antidote. Operatives are therefore advised to be extremely careful when handling these darts. People have died from as little as two micrograms of the poison – an amount five hundred times lighter than a grain of sand.

Thermite reaction

Golden poison frog – source of batrachotoxin

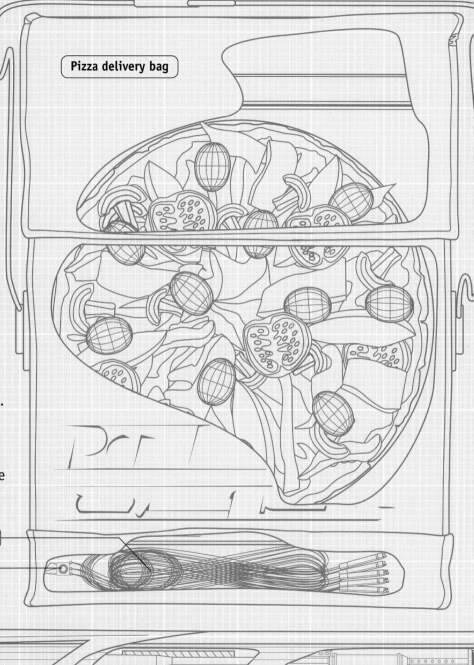

Pizza delivery bag

Thin metal wires

Piezoelectric crystal

Plastic blowgun

Scorpia

From: Smithers (Covert Weapons Section)
To: Everyone, R&D
Subject: Scorpia

You may be aware of the recent activities of the criminal group known as Scorpia. Some of the equipment recently issued to one of their agents is now being researched here at MI6 (documentation follows); here is a brief introduction for those of you who are unfamiliar with this organization.

Taking its name from its four main fields of activity – sabotage, corruption, intelligence and assassination – Scorpia has flourished since it was set up in the early 1980s. It is responsible for a tenth of the world's terrorism, which it undertakes on a contract basis. We suspect its involvement in several major ecological disasters, countless murders, and political manipulation on a massive scale.

Scorpia is led by a small council of ex-government spies and assassins, drawn from the intelligence services of many nations. There were twelve founder members, but now only seven remain. It maintains a training centre on the island of Malagosto near Venice, where promising students are taught espionage, survival and, more importantly, how to kill; a large portion of Scorpia's income comes from contract murders.

Scorpia agents should always be considered armed and dangerous, even after a thorough search, as much of their R&D budget goes on the development of concealed weaponry.

Smithers

Pizza Delivery Assassin Kit [1]

Scorpia sent Alex to kill the deputy head of MI6 Special Operations, Mrs Jones. He gained access to her heavily guarded apartment building disguised as a pizza delivery boy.

The olives on the four seasons pizza were in fact soundless explosives for destroying locks, and made short work of Mrs Jones's front door. The guard was already unconscious, a victim of Scorpia's fastest-acting knockout drug, which was administered by a blowgun disguised as a drinking straw.

Lift indicator plate: Although it is a very specialized device, this has been used surprisingly often by Scorpia operatives on assassination missions. It is designed to replace the indicator panel on the outside of a lift, and fool an observer into thinking that the lift is stopping on an earlier or later floor than it really is.

The plate, which is magnetic, is attached over the real indicator board. Placing it on a metal surface completes an electrical circuit which activates the device. A tiny watch battery, a simple silicon chip and a series of lights are built into the back of the plate. As the lift rises, the chip tells the numbers to light up slightly more or less quickly than usual, and to stop in a pre-programmed place.

The plate is thin, light and flexible, and by adding a label it is easy to disguise it as a card, leaflet or flyer.

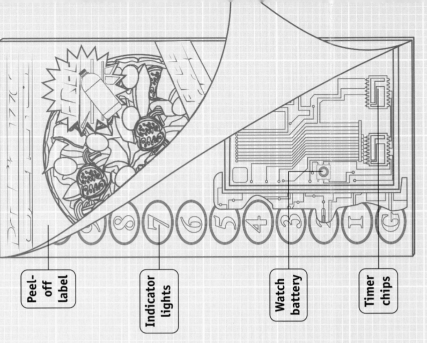

- **Peel-off label**
- **Indicator lights**
- **Watch battery**
- **Timer chips**

Pistol concealed in soft-drink bottle: The bottle comes in two parts, joined together in the middle. When the top and bottom are twisted apart, the catch releases and the contents can be removed.

Concealed within the bottle is a waterproof package, the same colour as the surrounding liquid. The package contains a slim, extremely lightweight semi-automatic pistol with a seven-shot magazine. To keep the weight down even further, Scorpia assassination agents are often issued with just enough ammunition to complete their assignments.

With the bottle assembled and filled, it looks, feels and weighs almost the same as a real bottle of soft drink; the lid can even be unscrewed and some of the liquid poured out before the package is revealed.

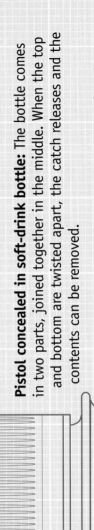

- **Conventional screw cap**
- **Soft drink**
- **Waterproof bag**

Exploding olives: The olives on the pizza are in fact small thermite charges. The outer shell is thin but tough and flexible; it is made of black plastic disguised to look like a slightly greasy, sticky olive. It contains a small amount of smokeless gunpowder packed around a plastic bag. This bag in turn contains a mixture of powdered aluminium and iron oxide.

A plastic box in the false bottom of the pizza bag contains a piezoelectric crystal similar to those used in gas cigarette lighters; when squeezed it produces enough current to create a spark. Unlike a battery, it has no metal parts, and so does not risk setting off metal detectors. The very thin metal wires running out of the box should also be undetectable.

The "olives" are stuck and squashed into place and one of the wires is then jabbed through the plastic shell. A button on the capacitor box squeezes the crystal and creates a high-voltage charge through the wires. A spark jumps between the two ends and ignites the smokeless powder. This causes enough heat to start the thermite reaction.

The aluminium and iron oxide mixture burns at a temperature of more than 3,000 degrees Celsius and will cut through any metal in a matter of seconds.

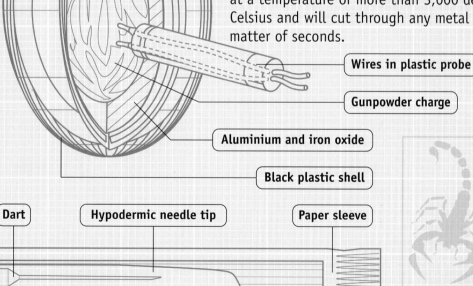

Wires in plastic probe

Gunpowder charge

Aluminium and iron oxide

Black plastic shell

Dart

Hypodermic needle tip

Paper sleeve

Blowgun:Olives
N103:N104 TANKER

Pizza Delivery Assassin Kit [2]

The front entrance to Mrs Jones's apartment building was guarded by two MI6 agents with a metal detector. In order to smuggle a gun through the sensors, it was concealed inside a bottle of soft drink. Alex had only to leave it on the front desk, step through the detector and pick it up on the other side.

The special offers card he carried was actually a fake indicator panel for the lift. Stuck magnetically over the real one, it fooled the agents into thinking that Alex had gone to a different floor.

Invisible Sword: Scorpia's terrifying new weapon is based on a technological marvel: the nanoshell. Each one is a thousand times smaller than the tip of a human hair and consists of a thin coating of gold around a polymer bead containing hydrogen cyanide. When the nanoshells are injected into the victim's body, a protein bonded to the gold coating guides them to the heart, where they accumulate. If the gold remains unbroken, the shells are harmlessly eliminated from the body within the space of a month. However, terahertz beams – high-frequency radio waves – will cause the gold coating to break down and release the cyanide directly into the heart. Death occurs in a matter of minutes. Having contaminated thousands of children's regular immunizations with nanoshells, Scorpia built a hot-air balloon to carry terahertz dishes over London and bathe the population in the beams.

The balloon itself was painted blue and white to blend in with the sky. Hanging from it was a plastic platform carrying four dishes, one at each corner to give as wide a coverage as possible for the terahertz shower.

A nanodevice activates in the human bloodstream

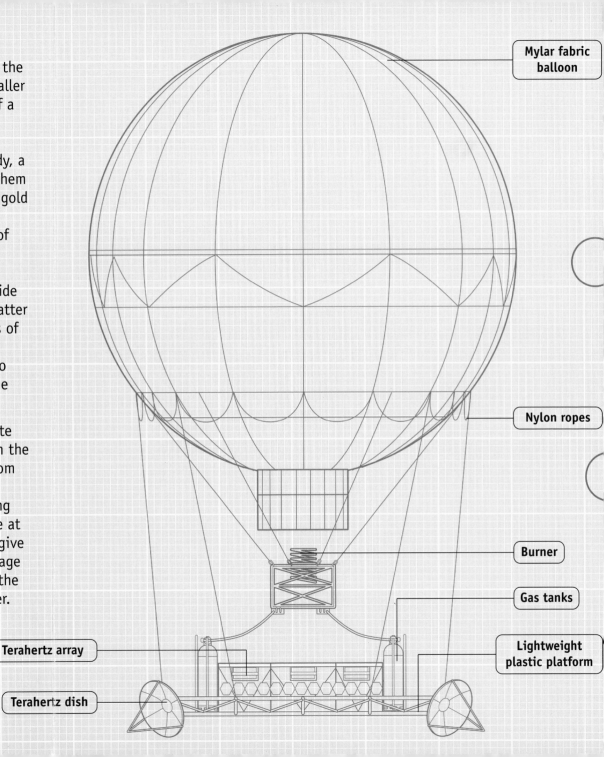

Mylar fabric balloon

Nylon ropes

Burner

Gas tanks

Lightweight plastic platform

Terahertz array

Terahertz dish

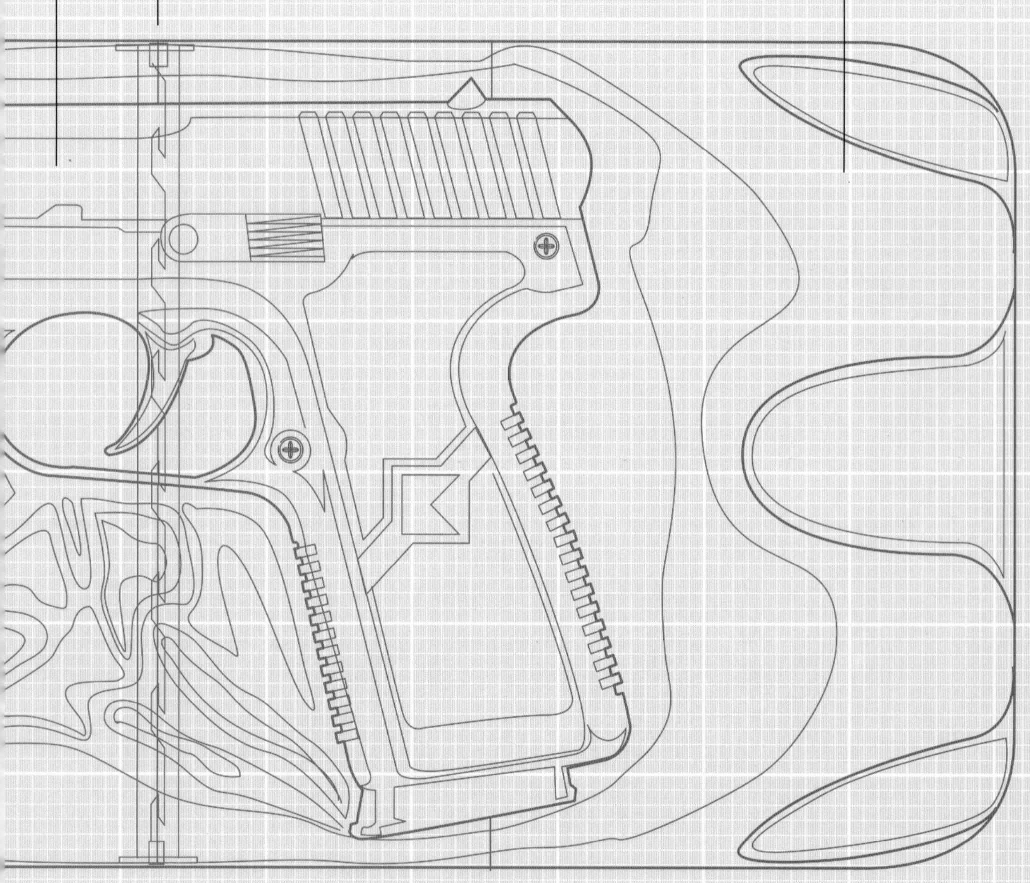

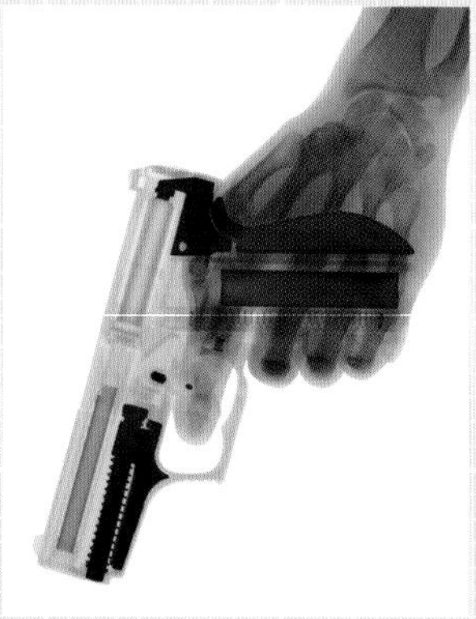

Pistol
Catch (hidden under label)
Bottle end cap

Security X-ray of a semi-automatic pistol

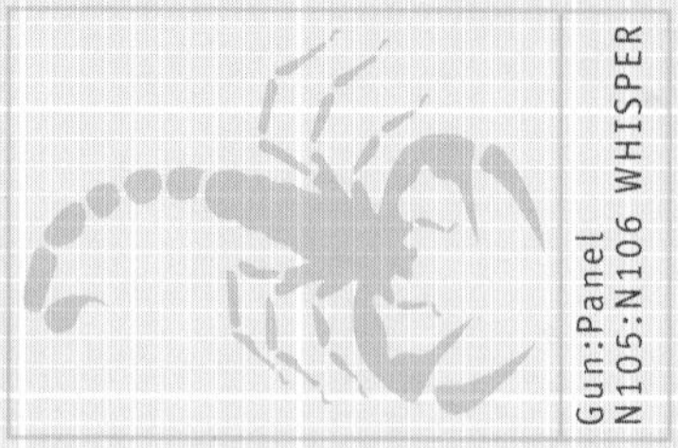

Gun:Panel
N105:N106 WHISPER

Operation Invisible Sword

Scorpia's master plan involved a new and terrifying weapon code-named Invisible Sword. It was based on cutting-edge nanotechnology: a branch of science dealing with objects so small they can only be seen with scanning electron microscopes. Nanotechnology is already all around us – in windows, car tyres, even lipstick – and its widespread use to make weapons as deadly and mysterious as this cannot be far away.

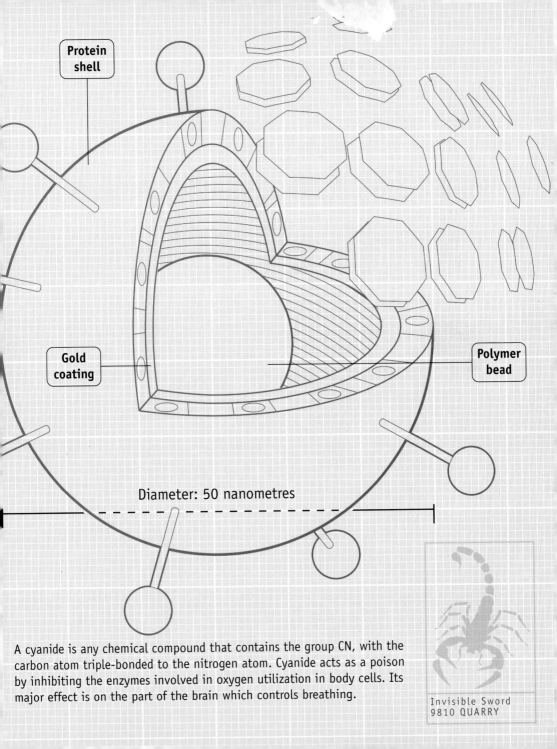

Protein shell

Gold coating

Polymer bead

Diameter: 50 nanometres

A cyanide is any chemical compound that contains the group CN, with the carbon atom triple-bonded to the nitrogen atom. Cyanide acts as a poison by inhibiting the enzymes involved in oxygen utilization in body cells. Its major effect is on the part of the brain which controls breathing.

Invisible Sword
9810 QUARRY

Glossary

Key scientific and technical terms used in this book

ABS resin A type of plastic used to make many different types of products, from pipes to golf-club heads to children's toys. ABS has excellent shock absorbance and is resistant to low temperatures.

Advanced encryption standard (AES) Encryption means making information unreadable unless it is known how to decode it. The advanced encryption standard is a particular way of doing this which has been chosen for use by the United States government; it is considered by experts to be extremely secure, and is relatively easy to use.

Antenna An electronic component designed to send or receive radio waves. Most antennas are simple rods or loops of metal or wire.

Burst transmission A radio transmission that compresses a large amount of information into a short time. Often used by the military to minimize the chance of signals being detected.

Candela (cd) A measure of brightness or intensity of light. An ordinary wax candle produces approximately one candela.

Capacitor A device that stores energy in an electric field. Capacitors can be used like a fast battery and are often used to keep power supply smooth and even.

Central processing unit (CPU) This is the part of a computer that carries out the instructions of the computer program.

Decibel (dB) A measure of sound pressure – often used to describe how loud something is. 10 dB is about as loud as a person's breathing sounds from three metres away; 80 dB is a vacuum cleaner from one metre; 120 dB is a loud rock concert. At 130 dB, sounds begin to hurt. At 190 dB they can cause ruptured eardrums, and sounds of 200 dB or more can even kill.

Electromagnet A type of magnet made by passing an electric current through a coil of wire.

Electromagnetic (EM) spectrum The name for the collection of all the different types of EM radiation – waves which carry energy from one place to another. Light is one kind – the only part of the spectrum we can see.

Size of a wavelength: House | CD disk | This dot | Cell | Bacteria | Virus | Protein | Water molecule

RADIO WAVES — INFRARED — ULTRAVIOLET — "HARD" X-RAYS

MICROWAVES — VISIBLE — "SOFT" X-RAYS — GAMMA RAYS

The spectrum ranges from low-frequency, long-wavelength waves such as radio waves, to microwaves (including terahertz waves), then infrared, visible light (from red through to violet), ultraviolet light, X-rays and gamma rays (very high-frequency waves) with very short wavelengths.

Enzyme A type of chemical that speeds up chemical reactions. Our bodies contain many different kinds of enzyme to help digest food or to contract and relax our muscles.

Fullerene Amazing though it is, diamond (the hardest mineral known to man) and graphite (the soft substance that makes up pencil leads) are both forms of carbon. The difference is in the shape of the molecules and the way they are bonded together. Fullerene molecules, discovered in the late twentieth century, are atoms of carbon arranged into spheres, tubes or rings.

Geiger counter A device for measuring levels of ionizing radiation – often used for detecting the dangerous radiation given off by the materials used in nuclear reactors and atomic bombs.

Generator A device which turns mechanical energy – such as the spinning of a turbine – into electrical energy.

Head-up display (HUD) Head-up displays, or HUDs, are ways of displaying information to a person in such a way that it is overlaid on what they see, and is always present in their visual field whichever way they look. Jet pilots, for example, can have flight information projected onto their visors, which means they do not have to look away to check their instruments.

High-tensile materials Tension is a force on a material that puts it under strain – a stretching force as opposed to a squeezing force (compression). Tensile strength is a measure of the maximum amount of tension a material can undergo before it breaks. So high-tensile materials can stand large amounts of tension without damage.

Infrared The part of the EM spectrum just below visible light is infrared, which means "below red", just as ultraviolet means "above violet". Objects at room temperature or above emit infrared radiation, emitting more the hotter they are. This cannot be seen with the naked eye, but can be picked up with a special camera or receiver. The many uses for infrared light include night vision equipment (hot objects, like people, will show up more brightly than their surroundings) and remote control units.

Magnesium A silvery-white lightweight metal, magnesium ignites when exposed to air and burns with a dazzling white flame.

Mercury switch Mercury is a metal which is liquid at room temperature. In a mercury tilt switch, a blob of the metal is contained in a glass bulb. At either end, there is a pair of electrical contacts. If the switch is tilted, and mercury rolls down to either end, it will complete the circuit.

Nanofibre Fibres made from tiny carbon nanotubes – rolled-up sheets of graphite fifty thousand times thinner than a human hair. Some types of nanofibre are thought to be the world's toughest material.

Nanotechnology One nanometre is one millionth of a millimetre. Scientists have recently begun thinking about machines of around this scale – from 0.1 to 100 nanometres. Some simple machines have already been made, including gears and motors.

Nylon A strong, flexible type of plastic often made into fibres and ropes.

Piezoelectric effect Certain crystals, when squeezed, produce an electrical voltage. This effect is also reversible; applying an electrical voltage to the crystal can cause it to change shape slightly. Some cigarette lighters use a piezoelectric crystal – it is squeezed to provide the electric spark that lights the gas. Quartz crystals in many watches and clocks use this effect to create a series of pulses, keeping the clock ticking regularly.

Plastic explosive Developed shortly before the Second World War, plastic explosives are soft, easy to mould into shape, and are safe over a wider range of temperatures than other explosives.

Polycarbonate A tough, durable form of plastic that can be moulded once heated up. Products made from it include sunglasses lenses, compact discs and even bulletproof glass.

Polytetrafluoroethylene (PTFE) A material which is often used as a non-stick coating for pans and other cookware. It has the lowest coefficient of friction of any solid substance known to man – which is another way of saying that it is very slippery.

Polyurethane elastomer A rubbery material containing many tiny cells.

Radioactivity Some materials – called radioactive isotopes – decay naturally over time, giving off various particles or rays in the process. This radiation can be extremely dangerous to living creatures as it can destroy or alter the cells of the body. Radioactive isotopes such as uranium-235 and plutonium-239 are used in nuclear weapons.

Ramjet A type of jet engine designed to work at very high speeds, so that air is forced into the front of the engine; ramjets do not work well at speeds of less than six hundred miles per hour. They are lightweight and contain no major moving parts.

Scanning electron micrograph (SEM) An ordinary microscope works by bouncing a beam of light off the object being studied; a scanning electron microscope uses a beam of electrons. Because electrons have a much shorter wavelength, it is able to see much finer detail. Some of the pictures in this book have been taken in this way, and so are referred to as scanning electron micrographs.

Schlieren photography A method for photographing the flow of air (or other compressible fluids) around objects. It is useful in aircraft or car design to help make the vehicle aerodynamic.

Solar panels Devices which convert light into electricity.

Terahertz waves One hertz means "once per second"; one terahertz means "one thousand billion times per second". Terahertz waves are high-frequency radio waves, similar to microwaves, which cycle one thousand billion times a second.

Thermite reaction A chemical reaction, involving aluminium and (usually) iron oxide, which produces intense heat.

Titanium A metal which is as strong as steel but 45% lighter, and highly resistant to corrosion. Often mixed with other metals to form titanium alloys, it is used in the manufacture of aircraft, missiles and everyday products such as golf clubs and bicycles.

Universal serial bus (USB) USB cables and ports are a common way of connecting modern computer devices, such as mice, printers and cameras, to computers.

Ultra wide-band (UWB) radar A type of radar which can be used to see through walls; it is being developed for use by the military and the police.

Collect all six Alex Rider™ novels:

STORMBREAKER 1-84428-092-6

 POINT BLANC 1-84428-093-4

SKELETON KEY 1-84428-094-2

 EAGLE STRIKE 1-84428-095-0

SCORPIA 0-7445-7051-4

 ARK ANGEL 0-7445-8324-1

Also available on tape and CD, read by Oliver Chris